mondo and the magic horn

Mondo and the Magic Horn

Shiko Nguru
Sawyer Cloud

Collins

Contents

Five facts about Kenya 2

Chapter 1 4

African horn instruments 14

Chapter 2 16

Kenya then and now 26

Chapter 3 28

Umoja Day 36

Chapter 4 38

Traditional jewellery 46

Chapter 5 48

African musical instruments 58

Chapter 6 60

About the author 70

About the illustrator 72

Book chat 74

Five facts about Kenya

1. Many of the world's fastest long distance runners have come from Kenya. Kenyan runners have won over 100 Olympic medals!

2. Kenya's national animal is the lion. Kenya is home to over 2,500 lions!

3. The oldest known human fossil, around 1.5 million years old, was found in Kenya.

4. Football is Kenya's most popular sport. The Kenyan national football team is called the Harambee Stars.

5. Britain is the biggest importer of Kenyan tea. Kenya produces some of the best tea in the world.

Africa

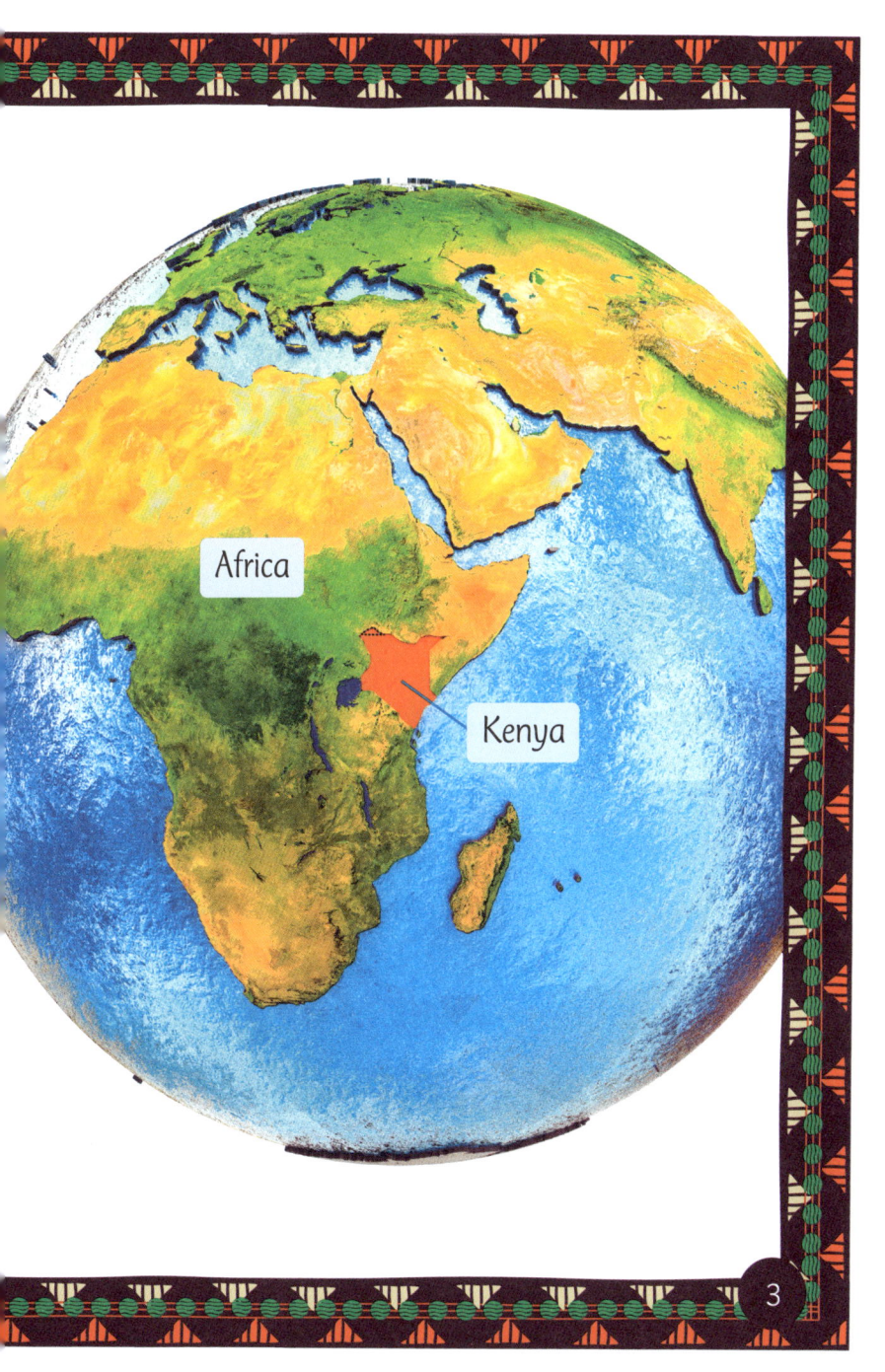

Kenya

Chapter 1

Mondo ran behind the sofa and crouched down. "Paka, come find me!" he shouted.

Paka was Mondo's pet cat. She was brilliant at hide-and-seek. It was the game Paka and Mondo both loved best.

Mondo stayed very still and tried not to giggle or breathe too loudly as he waited. A couple of minutes later, he heard a rustle above him. He looked up and there was Paka! She was perched on the sofa, staring down at him.

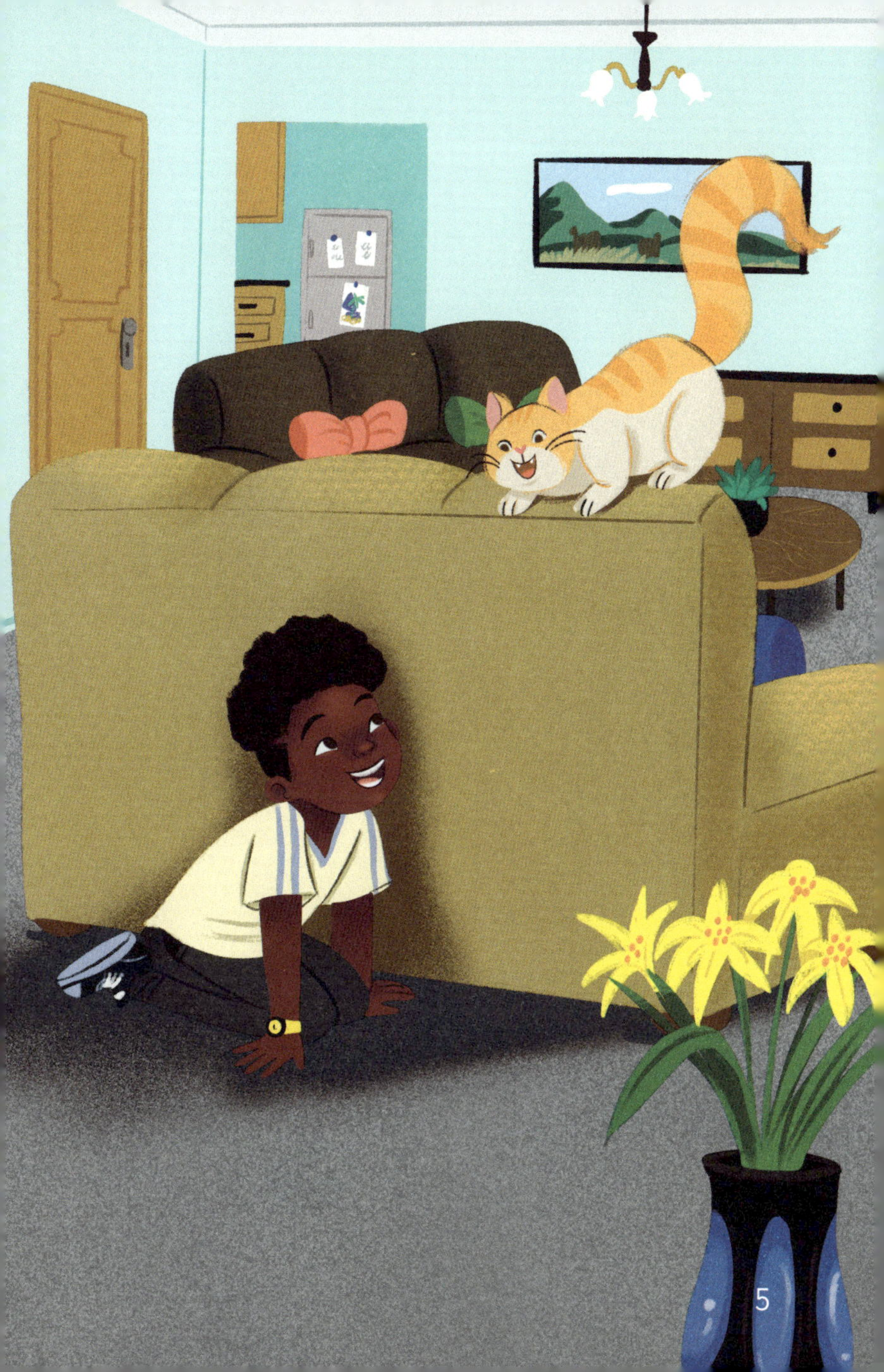

"You found me," he said, scooping her into his arms. Paka meowed proudly as Mondo petted her furry head.

"Mondo, it's time to do your chores," Mama announced from the kitchen.

"But we're playing hide-and-seek," Mondo complained. He hated doing chores and didn't want to stop the game. He checked his watch. It was half past five in the evening. "Can I do my chores later?" he begged.

Mama poked her head into the living room. "You can continue playing *after* you tidy up and sweep the floors," she said.

"Chores are such a bore!" Mondo whined.

"Chores may be a bore, but everyone has to do them," Mama tried to persuade him.

Mondo shook his head sadly. "I guess we can play tomorrow," he said to Paka, setting her down.

She trotted after him as he went up the stairs to get a broom.

He had just stepped into the hallway when he heard a sound.

TOOT! TOOT!

It sounded like a trumpet.

TOOT! TOOT!

The trumpeting was coming from inside the spare wardrobe. Mondo dashed towards it to investigate.

It was full of brooms, mops, boxes and buckets. He searched but couldn't find anything that could have made such a noise.

Then he heard it again. *TOOT! TOOT!*

Paka jumped between two buckets, then started to paw at something lying on the floor.

"What is it, Paka? What did you find?" Mondo asked as he went inside to get a better look.

"It's an animal horn!" he cried out excitedly.

The horn felt light when he seized it from the floor, and once it was in his hand, it began to vibrate.

Is this what was making that sound?
Mondo wondered.

Paka rubbed her head against his leg, as if to say he was right.

The horn continued to jiggle mysteriously in Mondo's hand, making him curious. Why was it vibrating? And could it really make a sound like a trumpet all on its own?

He decided to give it a test. Holding it firmly with both hands, he placed the narrow end on his lips and blew hard on it.

TOOOOOOT!

A strong gust of wind whooshed out of
the animal horn. It circled around Mondo's legs and
whisked him up into the air. It whisked Paka up too.

"What's happening?" Mondo shouted.

The wind spun them right up to the ceiling. It was as if they had been caught up in a small tornado.

Faster and faster they spun. Mondo hugged Paka under his arm and squeezed his eyes shut. It was so scary!

Suddenly, the little tornado stopped and everything went very still. Mondo felt his feet land gently on the ground.

When he opened his eyes, he found that he wasn't in the hallway anymore. He wasn't even in his house!

Mondo was right in the middle of a dense, green jungle.

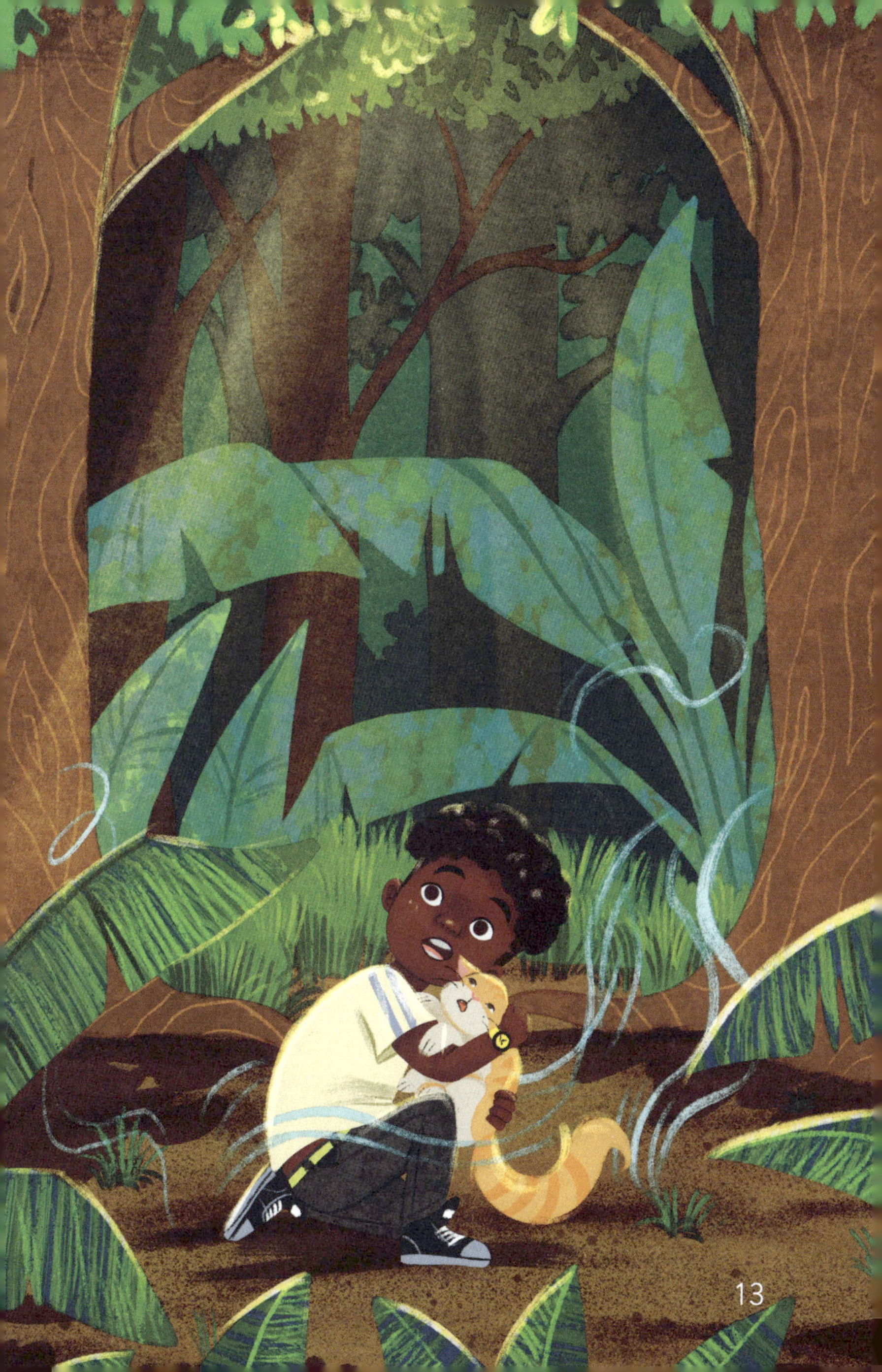

African horn instruments

Horns have been used across Africa for thousands of years. They are still used today.

African horn trumpets can be made from the horns of many different animals, such as antelopes and cows.

Some have holes on the side, others have holes in the end. They are used to send messages, announce events or make music.

cow horn

Here are some examples.

an antelope horn trumpet

a cow horn instrument

Chapter 2

Mondo was surrounded by tall trees and thick bushes, a palette of greens. The jungle was alive with the rhythmic sounds of insects humming and birds singing. He could almost taste the earthy air when he breathed in, a mixture of fragrant flowers and woody bark.

"Where are we?" Mondo asked.

"I don't know," Paka replied.

Mondo jumped in surprise. "Paka, you can talk!"

Paka's eyes were as wide as Mondo's. "You can understand me?"

Mondo nodded, staring down at the horn in his hand. "It must be the horn! First it carried us to this jungle, and now it's allowing us to speak to each other!"

"It's a magic horn!" Paka guessed.

Mondo beamed as he stuffed the horn safely into his pocket. He had read a lot of books about magical objects and had always wanted one.

The sound of feet crunching through dry foliage alerted them to people nearby. The footsteps were getting louder as the group headed their way.

"Quick, over here!" Paka whispered, scurrying behind a tree. Mondo crouched beside her.

A group of women and girls soon broke through the bushes, their silhouettes standing out against the lush vegetation. They were dressed in animal skins with large pots balanced on their heads.

Mondo gasped. "We've travelled back in time to the olden days! They look just like the people from our history books. This is how people dressed in ancient Kenya!"

19

"Shhhh!" Paka hushed him, but it was too late, a girl from the group had heard them.

"Hi Mondo, hi Paka," she greeted them warmly.

Mondo and Paka exchanged confused looks. How did the girl know their names? It must be part of the horn's magic.

"Hi," they replied, warily stepping out from behind the tree.

"You'd better hurry," she said. "We're taking these pots to get water from the river, but there are plenty more jobs to do before Umoja Day. Everyone must do their part, you know!"

"What's Umoja Day?" Paka asked, but the girl had already disappeared into the foliage.

"I don't know what Umoja Day is, Paka, but I'd love to find out," Mondo said. He marched off towards the girl.

They soon came upon a little village that was buzzing with activity. The houses were made from mud with thatched grass roofs. They were arranged in a neat circle with a wide, open space in the middle.

The village was filled with people working. There were men pulling large bulls into sheds and women weaving colourful baskets. Even the hens clucked contentedly as they laid big eggs. Everyone seemed happy as they went about their work.

23

"Excuse me, please. What is Umoja Day?" Mondo asked.

A man carrying a bow and arrows stopped to reply. "Umoja is a Swahili word that means 'togetherness'. Umoja Day is when people from the local villages come together to trade their goods."

"It's called barter trade. Each community trades what they have for something different that they need," a girl said. "Our village trades bulls and baskets for vegetables and honey."

"That's right, Amani. And there's lots to do before the people get here. You'd better find your age group and get to work!" the man said.

Mondo started to feel excited. He liked the idea of having an important job. "What does my age group do?"

Amani pulled his hand. "Come with me. I'll show you!"

Kenya then and now

In the olden days, children in Kenya learned through apprenticeship. They learned skills like basket weaving, hunting and farming from older members of the community.

These days, children in Kenya learn subjects like maths, science and literature from teachers in schools.

Chapter 3

Amani led Mondo and Paka to the far side of the village. They saw lots of groups together doing different jobs.

Amani waved at a group of girls. "That's my sister Amara and *her* age group. They're all between 13 and 15."

Amara's group was busy using rocks to grind grain into flour. They sang songs as they pushed the stones back and forth to the rhythm of their voices.

"After harvesting grain from the fields, they grind it into flour," Amani explained.

"The flour can be traded for salt from another village. It's a very important job."

"I'd love to try," Mondo said. He knelt in front of a flat rock with grain heaped on top of it. Using a large stone, he began to grind the grain into flour, copying the girls.

Mondo knew that flour was an ingredient in bread, cakes and lots of other foods. "Grinding grain is a very important job," he puffed. It was hard work, and beads of sweat popped up on his nose.

"Yes, but it's not your job," Amani said, pulling him away.

Nearby was a group of older boys cleaning various tools and weapons. They were cracking jokes while they worked.

Amani waved at the boys. "This age group works on making farm tools, arrows and spears. We keep what we need and trade the rest for clay pots."

"I'd love to try!" Mondo said. He picked up a large shovel and began to clean it. It was very heavy!

Mondo understood how necessary tools and weapons were. They were used for farming, building and hunting. "Making tools is certainly a very important job," he wheezed, already exhausted.

"Yes, but it's not your job," Amani said, handing the shovel back to one of the boys. She tugged at Mondo's arm, guiding him to an area where a group of young girls were seated.

"This is *my* age group," Amani said. "Our job is to make jewellery using beads."

Mondo's eyes sparkled as he took in the brilliant-coloured beads. There were bracelets and anklets spread all around.

Amani sat down and began to thread beads. "We make these for the women and girls to wear on Umoja Day."

"I'd love to try!" Mondo said. He plopped down and picked up a piece of string. As carefully as he could, he worked to thread a series of colourful beads. After a while, Mondo stopped to observe his work.

His face glowed as he admired the bracelet he had made. "Jewellery-making is a tricky but very important job," Mondo said.

"Yes, but it's not your job. The boys in *your* age group are over there," Amani pointed. "That's where you need to be."

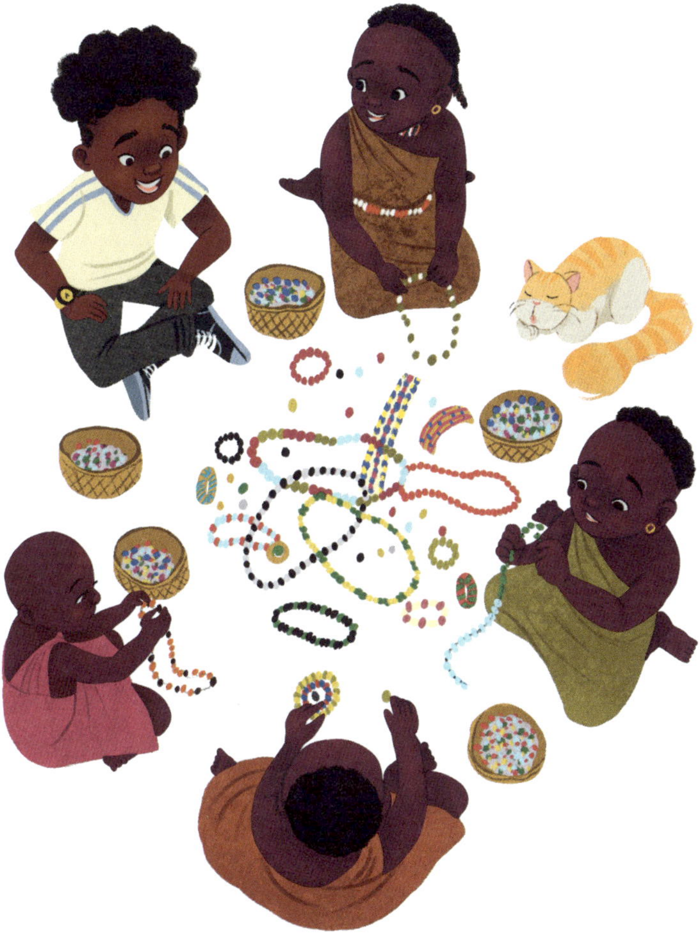

"What do you think my job will be, Paka?" Mondo asked.

"I don't know. But whatever it is, I'm sure it will be just as important as all the other jobs," Paka replied.

"Mondo, over here!" beckoned a boy who looked around ten years old.

He and a group of boys were collecting sticks, picking them off the ground.

"Our age group's job is to collect sticks," the boy said proudly.

Mondo's heart sank. "That's it? We collect sticks?"

It didn't sound very important. In fact, it reminded Mondo of his chores back at home.

"Chores are a bore," Mondo grumbled to Paka as he slowly began to pick up sticks.

Umoja Day

Umoja means togetherness or unity.

In many rural communities, there is a day set aside once a month, for people to come together and trade items. They are usually called Market Days.

Market Day is a time of community celebration too, with music, food and entertainment.

Chapter 4

The scorching sun made Mondo's skin prickle. Sweat dripped from his forehead as he loaded sticks into his arms.

"Picking up sticks is exhausting – and boring," Mondo whined.

"Look! They're doing something fun over there. Why don't you join in?" Paka persuaded him.

The boys in Mondo's group were playing a game. They'd divided themselves into two teams to see who could collect the most sticks. One of the boys counted while the others raced to add sticks to their team's pile.

"I'd love to try!" Mondo piped up. He joined one of the teams and began to compete. The teams spread out all over the village, racing this way and that, scooping up as many sticks as they could find.

Mondo rushed around, feeling exhilarated.
He cheered and whooped as he helped his team.
"To be honest, I never thought picking up sticks would be such fun!" he told Paka.

When time was up, the teams counted the sticks.
Mondo's team had collected the most.
They were victorious!

"Now it's time to sort the sticks. We need to separate the big ones from the small ones," the boys announced.

They got to work sorting the sticks. It was a huge heap.

"It's going to take hours to sort through all these," Mondo observed.

"We'll use the togetherness of Umoja. By working together, we'll get it done in no time," one of the boys said.

Together, they started comparing and separating big sticks from small ones. They even made up a game where two boys would close their eyes and pick a stick from the pile. Whoever had the bigger stick when they opened their eyes won.

Before long, they had sorted through the whole pile of sticks. "That didn't take as long as I thought!" Mondo told Paka.

"Now it's time to carry all these to the village centre," the boys told Mondo. They tied the sticks into bundles. Each boy picked up a bundle and placed it on his head. Forming a line, they sang as they marched towards the village centre.

"I'd love to try!" Mondo chirruped. He placed a bundle on his head and joined the march. The song they sang had the same tune as the alphabet song, but the words were in the Swahili language.

Sisi ni vijana,
Tunabeba vijiti.

(We are young boys,
We are carrying sticks)

Sisi ni vijana,
Tunabeba vijiti.

Once at the village centre, they arranged the bundles in order of size. One by one, the villagers came to collect them.

"These big sticks will help build containers for our grain," the older girls said.

"These small sticks will be perfect for making arrows," the older boys said.

"We need big sticks to build extra sheds for the bulls," the men said.

"We need small sticks to hang our baskets," the women said.

"And our jewellery!" Amani added.

It seemed like everyone needed the sticks that Mondo's group had collected. Mondo felt proud that he'd helped the community in such a major way.

"You were right, Paka. Picking sticks *is* an important job, just like the rest," Mondo beamed.

"Maybe the most important job of all," Paka remarked.

Just then, loud drumming filled the air. Villagers started to pour into the centre, singing and dancing in rhythm to the drumbeats.

"What's happening?" Mondo asked.

"It's time for the Umoja Day celebration to start!" Amani cheered.

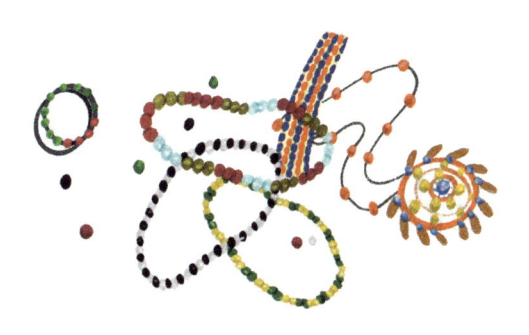

Traditional jewellery

Beaded jewellery has a long history in Kenya, dating back to the early 19th century. Beads were made from materials like clay, shells, ivory and bone.

47

Chapter 5

A troop of drummers seized sticks from the piles as they filed into the village. They used the sticks to beat their drums and lead the villagers in a song. Boys and girls in Mondo's age group formed a little train and danced around the drummers.

They sang and waved branches as they welcomed the visitors and guests for Umoja Day. The beads worn by the women and girls jingled as they danced. The men and boys joined in by clashing sticks against the shields they carried.

"Karibu!" Amani yelled out to the visitors.

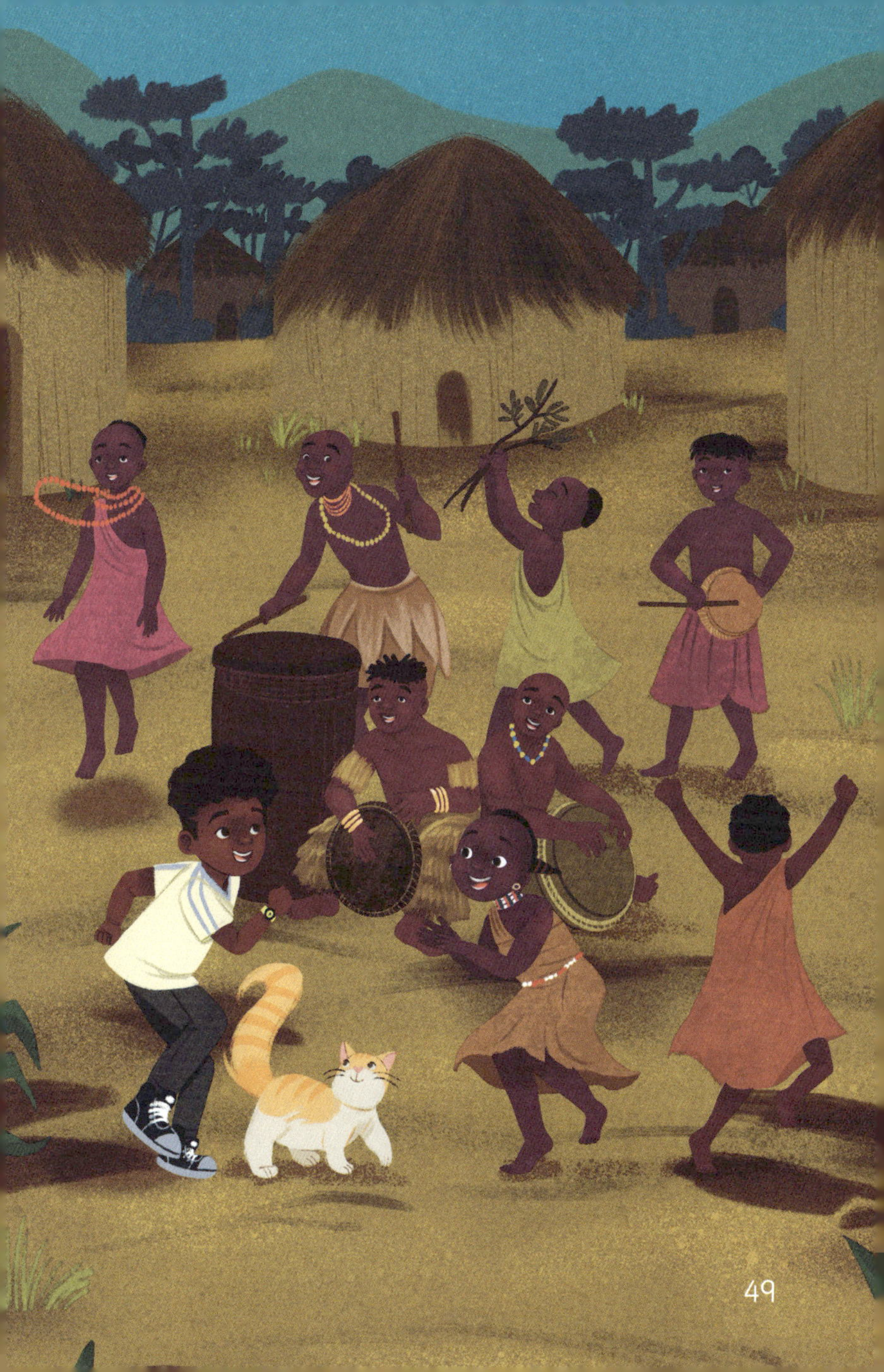

The last visitors filed into the village. Silence fell, as the village chief strode into the centre. "Umoja Day has begun!" he announced. "By sharing what we have made, I guarantee that we'll all have a good time!"

Members of the crowd set up a large open-air market. Mondo watched as villagers with milk and tea traded for arrows and farm tools. Every villager was trading and every village cart was filled to the brim with goods to take back home.

Mondo paused to breathe in the rich aromas of smoky meat and spicy vegetables. He drifted towards the smells. Platters of food were passed around, with everyone sharing. Mondo picked out a goat rib for himself and a fish for Paka. He added steaming vegetable rice to their banana-leaf plates.

Paka licked her paws. "That was delicious," she said, as Mondo nodded in agreement.

"Come on, Mondo, or you'll miss the games!" Amani called out.

51

Mondo followed to where a pair of boys were wrestling as people cheered. Both wrestlers jerked this way and that as they tried to pin each other to the ground.

Beside the wrestlers, a group of girls were playing a different sort of game. Players were taking turns dodging a ball made of animal skin that was being hurled at them by their opponents.

"Look, Mondo!!" Paka exclaimed.

Groups of men and women wearing wooden masks were making their way into the village centre. Some of their masks were playful, while others looked scary. The mask wearers leaped and twirled and chased people.

"Don't be scared," Mondo reassured Paka, "they're just playing." He carried Paka in his arms and joined the masked dancers.

In the end, it was a joyful day of dancing, trading, eating and playing games.

"Umoja Day wouldn't have been possible without everyone doing their part," Paka said.

Mondo smiled. "Every job was important. Even picking up sticks!"

TOOT! TOOT!

A sudden trumpeting sound made Mondo and Paka jump. It was the magic horn in Mondo's pocket. He pulled it out, staring at it curiously. "What do you think it wants us to do?"

TOOT! TOOT!

"Try blowing on it like you did the last time," Paka suggested.

55

Mondo lifted the horn to his mouth and blew.

TOOOOOOT!

A blast of air rushed out of the horn and formed a spinning cloud around them. It carried them up in the air and whipped them around and around as if they were on an invisible merry-go-round.

"It's happening again!" Mondo shouted. He was a little nervous, but not nearly as afraid as he was the last time.

"Where do you think we'll end up this time?" Paka yelled.

Mondo hugged her tight and closed his eyes. "No idea!"

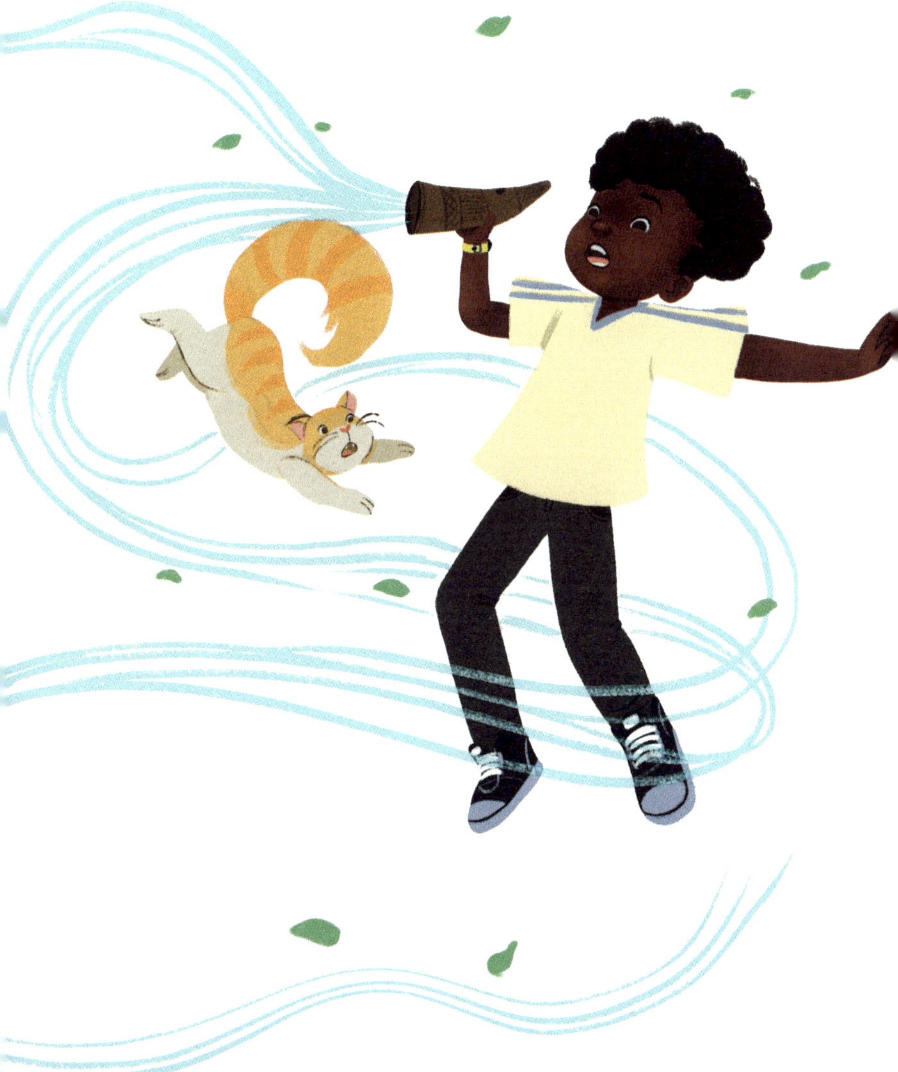

African musical instruments

Traditional African musical instruments include drums, rattles, horns and stringed instruments. Here are some.

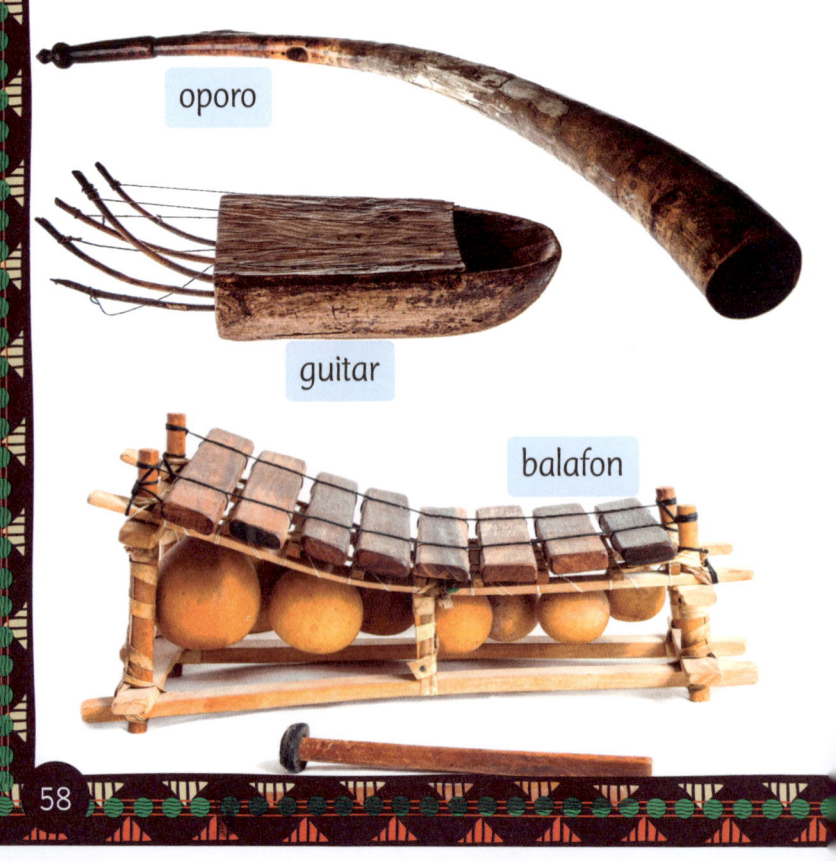

oporo

guitar

balafon

58

- udu
- kora
- frame drum
- harp
- dundun drum

Chapter 6

The spinning slowed and eventually stopped. Mondo's feet touched gently on the ground. And when he opened his eyes, he was back in the hallway. He checked his watch and it was still half past five.

The magic horn had transported them back to the exact same time and place they'd left from!

"We're back home, Paka!" Mondo exclaimed.

Paka purred and rubbed her cheek against his. Although she couldn't speak anymore, he could tell she was happy to be back home too.

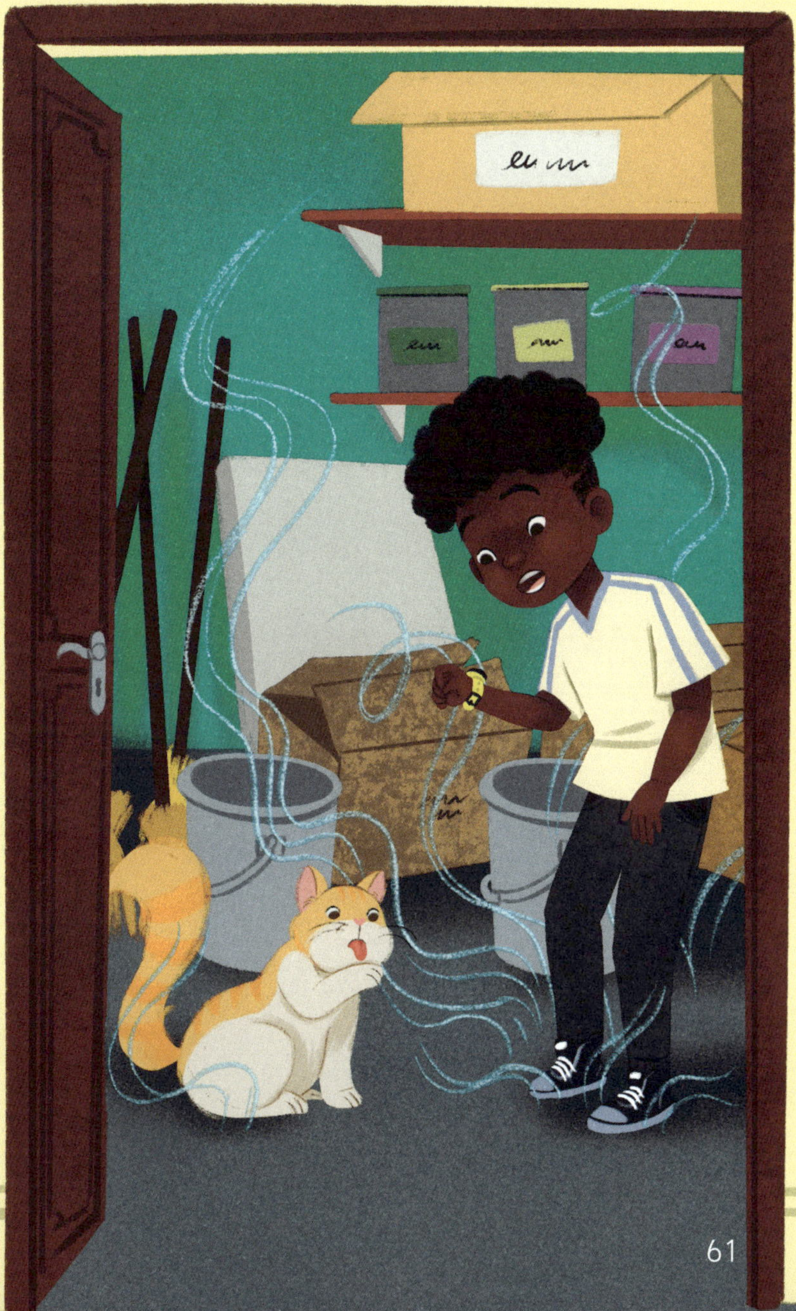

"There's no time to spare. I have important work to do," Mondo declared.

He grabbed some cleaning supplies. "Mama is counting on me to tidy up and sweep the floors."

Remembering the fun he had doing jobs in the village, Mondo challenged himself to tidy and clean the floor in under ten minutes.

He put on a playlist of the songs he loved best.

"Chores don't have to be a bore!" he sang out to Paka, grooving along to the music as he worked. The ten minutes were up just as Mondo launched the last toy into the box. "Done!" he shouted.

"Honey, I have a surprise for you!" Mama called warmly.

Mondo scurried down the stairs, following his nose to the delicious scent wafting in from the back garden.

"A barbecue!" Mondo chirped. The sight of juicy sausages sizzling alongside colourful vegetable kebabs made his mouth water.

Mama beamed. "Yes, because I guessed you might want a treat after your chores." She pointed at the horn poking out of his pocket. "Did you enjoy your adventure?"

Mondo took a sharp breath. "You know about the horn?"

"It used to carry me away on adventures, when I was your age," she said.

"It did? Really? How does the magic horn work?" Mondo asked, staring wide-eyed with a serious expression.

Mama spread their blanket on the grass and passed a full plate to Mondo. She put some chunks of sausage in Paka's bowl too before patting the blanket next to her.

"I'll tell you all about the magic horn when we've eaten," she announced with a playful twinkle in her eyes.

Tiny bright stars twinkled above them as they tucked into their barbecue dinner. Mondo waited eagerly for Mama to take her last bite. He couldn't wait to hear about the horn's magic.

Eventually, she dabbed her mouth with a napkin. "That horn has been in our family for many, many years. Only very special children can hear its call."

"Seriously? Wow!" Mondo whispered. "The horn thinks I'm special?"

"Yes!" Mama trilled. "It's been in that wardrobe for years, just waiting to take the next child on adventures."

"It took us to a village where we got to celebrate Umoja Day!" Mondo told her excitedly.

Mama nodded. "The magic horn takes children back in time to show them what life was like. It also makes sure you have friends on your adventure to help you!"

Mondo smiled fondly as he remembered Amani and the boys from his group. "When will I get to go on my next adventure?"

Then, before Mama could answer, he felt a buzz in his pocket and heard a familiar sound.

TOOT! TOOT!

Mondo plucked the horn out and looked up at Mama, who nodded. It was time to go again. Mondo picked up Paka and hugged her to his chest.

Mondo's magic horn was whisking him away on his next adventure.

About the author

My name is Shiko and I'm an author of children's books that celebrate my love for African culture. I enjoy writing stories that bring the beauty and magic of Africa to life, weaving in the spirit of adventure wherever I can.

Shiko Nguru

How did you come up with the idea for this book?

I've always loved the idea of time travel and wonder what life was like centuries ago. Writing this book gave me a chance to finally explore how different (and sometimes not so different!) life was then compared to now.

Does anything in this book relate to your own experiences?

I love history and would have loved to be Mondo! Travelling back in time is something I have dreamed of doing all my life. Until they invent time travel, or I find my own magic horn, I'll settle for writing about it.

Do you have a pet? If they could talk, what would you ask?

I have a dog called Loki and I'd love to ask him what he thinks of our family!

If you had a magic horn, where would you like to travel to and why?
I would want to travel back in time to see my great-great-great-grandmother when she was a little girl. I would love to know if she and I are the same in any way!

Have you ever celebrated Umoja Day?
Many communities in Kenya have a day of togetherness called Market Day that is similar to the Umoja Day described in the book. It's a time of celebration and sharing what we have with each other. I got to attend Market Day many times growing up when I visited the countryside with my family.

What do you hope readers will get from this book?
I hope readers will develop an interest in researching the old ways of life. What did children hundreds of years ago like to do for fun? What did they wear? What did they eat?

If you wrote another Mondo and Paka adventure, where would they go?
Mondo and Paka's next adventure might take them back in time to see how islanders stopped raiders from invading their land.

About the illustrator

What made you want to be an illustrator?

I've always been interested in magic and using my imagination to tell stories. As a child, I loved everything that was creative and used every tool I had to draw or make something. When I got older and learned that some adults are paid to have fun with pencils and paper, I was obsessed with the possibility of earning a living as an artist. So, I just made it happen after working as a teacher, a librarian and a video artist. Drawing for children is the best job!

Sawyer Cloud

What did you like best about illustrating this book?

Coming from an African country, I think it's important to make African history exciting to learn. I like how the book brings children back in time, to a world where life was simpler and more magical! This book also helps to keep culture alive; I really learned a lot about Kenyan history when I was working on this book.

What was the most difficult thing about illustrating this book?

The most difficult part was the research. I had to make sure I had the right references for all the different scenes in the past in Kenya. There aren't many resources on the internet about Africa in the past, so finding the right resources was really important.

Which character did you like best?

I like Mondo's Mum a lot! She's not only cute in appearance, she also has a big heart and is a caring mother.

Is there anything or anyone in the story that relates to your own experiences?

I live in an African country. I actually come from Madagascar which is a really big island. So, I can relate to the culture in the book. I also have a huge imagination and when I was a child, I believed I was able to travel in time.

Where would you like to go if you found a magic horn?

I would go to the place where I met all my friends when I was a child. I'd go back to when I lived in a small village in Madagascar, on a sunny summer day!

Book chat

Have you ever read a book like this before?

What did Mondo learn on his adventure?

Which part of the book did you like best and why?

If you had a magic horn, where would you like to go?

If you could ask the author or illustrator anything, what would you ask?

Did any of the characters change from the start of the story to the end?

If you could talk to an animal, which would you choose and what would you ask?

Book challenge:
Design your own magic horn and pet to take on an adventure.

![Collins Big Cat logo]

Published by Collins
An imprint of HarperCollins*Publishers*

The News Building
1 London Bridge Street
London SE1 9GF
UK

Macken House
39/40 Mayor Street Upper
Dublin 1
D01 C9W8
Ireland

Text © Shiko Nguru 2024
Design and illustrations © HarperCollins*Publishers*
Limited 2024

10 9 8 7 6 5 4 3 2 1

ISBN 978-0-00-868121-0

All rights reserved. No part of this publication may be reproduced, stored in a retrieval system, or transmitted in any form by any means, electronic, mechanical, photocopying, recording or otherwise, without the prior written permission of the Publisher or a licence permitting restricted copying in the United Kingdom issued by the Copyright Licensing Agency Ltd, 5th Floor, Shackleton House, 4 Battle Bridge Lane, London SE1 2HX.

British Library Cataloguing-in-Publication Data
A catalogue record for this publication is available from the British Library.

Download the teaching notes and word cards to accompany this book at:
http://littlewandle.org.uk/signupfluency/

Get the latest Collins Big Cat news at
collins.co.uk/collinsbigcat

Author: Shiko Nguru
Illustrator: Sawyer Cloud (Advocate Art)
Publisher: Laura White
Product manager and
   commissioning editor: Caroline Green
Series editor: Charlotte Raby
Development editor: Catherine Baker
Project manager: Emily Hooton
Copyeditor: Sally Byford
Proofreader: Catherine Dakin
Cover designer: Sarah Finan
Typesetter: 2Hoots Publishing Services Ltd
Production controller: Katharine Willard

Printed in the UK.

MIX
Paper | Supporting responsible forestry
FSC FSC™ C007454
www.fsc.org

This book is produced from independently certified FSC™ paper to ensure responsible forest management.

For more information visit: www.harpercollins.co.uk/green

Made with responsibly sourced paper and vegetable ink

Scan to see how we are reducing our environmental impact.

Acknowledgements
The publishers gratefully acknowledge the permission granted to reproduce the copyright material in this book. Every effort has been made to trace copyright holders and to obtain their permission for the use of copyright material. The publishers will gladly receive any information enabling them to rectify any error or omission at the first opportunity.

P2t Eric Isselee/Shutterstock, P2b Mr. SUTTIPON YAKHAM/Shutterstock, P3 Harvepino/Shutterstock, P14 Andre Silva Pinto/Shutterstock, P15t Alissa Everett/Alamy, P15b Eric Lafforgue/Alamy, P26tl Tina Manley/Alamy, P26tr Wayne Hutchinson/Alamy, P26b Images & Stories/Alamy, P27t Claudiovidri/Shutterstock, P27b USAID/Alamy, PP36-37 Christophe Courteau/Nature Picture Library/Science Photo Library, P46 BE&W agencja fotograficzna Sp. z o.o./Alamy, P47t Oleg Doroshenko/Alamy, P47c imageBROKER.com GmbH & Co. KG/Alamy, P47b Danita Delimont/Alamy, P58t Andre Silva Pinto/Shutterstock, P58c André Pinto/Alamy, P58b Anastasiya Adamovich/Shutterstock, P59tl HQ3DMOD/Shutterstock, P59tr Tarek Khouzam/Shutterstock, P59cl Aliye Aral/Shutterstock, P59bl Art Directors & TRIP/Alamy, P59br Lebrecht Music/Alamy.